ARCHITECTURE IN MICHIGAN

ARCHITECTURE IN MICHIGAN

a representative photographic survey
by WAYNE ANDREWS

WAYNE STATE UNIVERSITY

Wayne State University, Detroit, 1967

A Twenty-fifth Anniversary Book

ILLUSTRATIONS

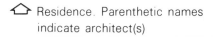 Residence. Parenthetic names
indicate architect(s)

ACKNOWLEDGMENTS

My first and deepest acknowledgment is to W. Hawkins Ferry. Twenty-three years ago, twenty years before I moved to Michigan, he was so kind as to introduce me to the architecture of our state, and year after year he continued the good work, driving my wife and me to towns that were not easily accessible before the era of the expressways. Mr. Ferry is the author of a forthcoming history of Detroit architecture (Wayne State University Press), which will be the first serious attempt to deal with any aspect of the buildings of Michigan.

And I should like to mention the terrifying efficiency of James M. Babcock, head of the Burton Historical Collection of the Detroit Public Library. Ostensibly Mr. Babcock is a librarian, but in reality he is the chief of a vast secret service of men and women all over Michigan who are dedicated to the problems of local history and will go to no end of trouble to help an author out. Thanks to Mr. Babcock and his friend in Ann Arbor, Mr. Herbert Bartlett, I had the good fortune to meet Mrs. Roger Hardenbergh of Manchester, who came graciously to my assistance in identifying old Manchester houses. Mrs. Dale C. Loveland of Grass Lake, Miss Dorothy Mitts of Port Huron and Mrs. Irving Nels Jorgenson of Grosse Pointe were also most helpful.

Finally, I should like to thank Dick Schuler and his remarkable staff at Compo Photo Service, New York, who made all the enlargements of my negatives used in this book. Besides giving my negatives every possible attention, Dick Schuler has given me invaluable photographic advice.

This is the first book to appear on the subject of architecture in Michigan. It surely will not be the last, and it is to be hoped that its failings will be excused by authorities in the years to come. It is in no sense an encyclopedic account, but a photographic survey whose aim is to be *representative:* that is, to include as many views as possible of buildings considered important either in their own time or in ours. Three drawings are reproduced, but the book consists of 105 photographs taken by the author. Two of these are of sculpture carved with architectural intent. The other 103 photographs are intended to show the progress of architecture from 1837, when Michigan was admitted to the Union, down to the present day.

Two-thirds of the photographs are of architecture in the 20th century. This is quite natural, for it was not until 1904, when Albert Kahn (1869-1942), a rabbi's son from Rhaunen in the German province of Westphalia, opened his own office in Detroit that the architecture of Michigan became of international importance.

"When I began," said Kahn, "the real architects would design only museums, cathedrals, capitals, monuments. The office boy was considered good enough to do factories. I'm still that office boy designing factories. I have no dignity to be impaired."

Kahn knew what he was talking about. He was an office boy himself in an architectural firm when he first arrived in Detroit at the age of ten. Later the sculptor Julius Melchers, father of the painter Gari Melchers, gave him drawing lessons on Sundays, and when not yet sixteen he went to work sketching for the firm of

Mason & Rice. For the first nine months he was on probation; after that he was given a salary of $30 a month.

He became, as all the world knows, the greatest factory architect in history.

By 1928 he was laying out a $40,000,000 tractor plant for the Soviet Union, not to mention $2,000,000,000 worth of other buildings in Russia, and by 1929 was receiving weekly orders for more than $1,000,000 worth of work. A staff of 400 was required, including 175 architectural designers. Kahn was not given to boasting but made it plain that his organization could provide the drawings for an impressive factory building in a week's time. There was no crossing or re-crossing of the production line in a Kahn design, and such items as flexible re-arrangement, excellent lighting, adequate ventilation, and low upkeep did not need to be discussed by his clients.

If this were the ideal book on Michigan architecture, Kahn's factories would be plentifully illustrated by the author's photographs. But such has been the expansion of Detroit as an industrial center that many of his most famous plants were altered or dismantled long ago. Even the Dodge Half-Ton Truck Plant of 1938 in Warren has been literally obliterated by recent changes.

"Evolution," Kahn was fond of reminding his clients, "is preferable to revolution." In his domestic work and in his educational and business buildings in Ann Arbor and Detroit, he proved he was one of the last of the eclectics, carrying on the magnificent tradition established by McKim, Mead & White in New York and D. H. Burnham in Chicago. Although the Packard plant of 1905 (Detroit's first reinforced concrete factory) may be one of his revolutionary achievements, Kahn the

evolutionist deserves equal attention. His own favorite building, the Clements Library at the University of Michigan, is here represented, as are the Main Library at Michigan and the Hill Auditorium (this last done in partnership with Ernest Wilby). Also emphasized are two of his mansions in Grosse Pointe, the residence of Edsel B. Ford (1929) and that of Alvan Macauley (1930). Nor is his contribution to the Detroit skyline neglected. The General Motors Building of 1920, followed by the Fisher Building of 1928, insured his reputation as a city planner.

Kahn was the first of the three architects who gave Michigan its international reputation. The second was Eliel Saarinen (1873-1950), a native of Helsingfors, Finland, who was called to Bloomfield Hills in 1925 after winning second prize in the competition for Tribune Tower, Chicago. Thanks to George Gough Booth, publisher of the

Detroit *News,* and his wife the former Ellen Warren Scripps, he was given the opportunity of designing Cranbrook School, the Cranbrook Academy of Art, the Cranbrook Institute of Science and, what may well be his masterpiece, the exquisite Kingswood School for Girls in the Cranbrook complex.

Saarinen was a provocative architect, challenging Americans with the gospel of the arts and crafts as taught in Finland. He was equally important as an educator, for he made the Cranbrook Academy of Art a center for instruction in architecture and the arts and crafts where the individual aims of the students were recognized and released. The Philadelphia city planner Edmund N. Bacon is a Cranbrook graduate. So is the Chicago architect Harry Weese, Jr. And the history of modern American furniture would be unwritten but for Florence Schust (later Mrs. Hans G. Knoll), Charles Eames, Eero Saarinen,

and Harry Bertoia, all of whom were Cranbrook-trained and Cranbrook teachers. Moreover, Bertoia's career as a sculptor may be said to have begun in the days he headed the Cranbrook metal-work studios.

Eliel's son, Eero Saarinen (1910-1961) completes the trinity of the great Michigan architects in our time. Although much of his work was erected beyond the borders of the state —the Dulles Airport at Chantilly, Virginia, the TWA Terminal at Kennedy, the CBS Building in New York City, the Ingalls Hockey Rink and the new colleges at Yale come instantly to mind, as does the John Deere headquarters at Moline, Illinois—it was here that he got his start. Taking over on his father's death the commission for the General Motors Technical Center at Warren, he demonstrated that he could be at once meticulous and amazing.

Like all great architects, Eero

Saarinen was dissatisfied. "Our architecture is too humble," he proclaimed. "It should be prouder, more aggressive, much richer and larger than we see it today. . . . We must explore and expand [our] horizons." He was no mean explorer himself. After digesting first his father's influence and then that of Miës van der Rohe, he took the risk of experimenting with sculptural forms and succeeded brilliantly in the TWA Terminal and elsewhere.

To Kahn and the two Saarinens must be given the credit for creating the atmosphere in which Marcel Breuer planned the Grosse Pointe Public Library, Ludwig Miës van der Rohe developed the Lafayette Park housing project, and Minoru Yamasaki plotted his course by conceiving the McGregor Community Conference Center at Wayne State University. And the most inventive firm of the 1960s,

Meathe, Kessler & Associates, might never have settled in Detroit but for the Kahn and Saarinen tradition. The most casual—and the most distinguished—example of domestic design in Michigan in recent years may be Meathe, Kessler's Swainson-Whitehead cottage at Manistee, completed in 1966.

But the architecture of Michigan does not *begin* with the first sketches of Albert Kahn. It begins in the 1830s and 1840s with the work of the often anonymous builders who fashioned the charming Gothic and Greek revival houses still to be seen at Grosse Ile, in Ann Arbor, and in smaller towns such as Marshall and Grass Lake. These unfortunately unknown men had already revealed what could be accomplished in the Romantic styles by the time the nation's leading designer of Gothic Castles and Italian Villas, Alexander Jackson Davis (1803-1892),

was approached in his New York office by his first Michigan clients. Davis' Gothic campus for the University of Michigan was destined to remain a dream, but he had the satisfaction of learning that three Italian Villas from his drafting board were executed in the Fort Street section of Detroit. This may be the proper place to lament the destruction of the Christopher Reeve house of 1852, the J. C. Boughman house of 1853, and the Bela Hubbard house of 1854.

Of course Detroit had its own professional architects in the Romantic era. The most talented may have been the English-born Gordon W. Lloyd (1832-1904), who was responsible not only for Christ Church, Detroit, but for the much more subtle Saint James Church on Grosse Ile. Among Lloyd's competitors the most ingenious appear to have been the brothers Octavius and Albert H.

Jordan from Hartford, Connecticut, creators of the Fort Street Presbyterian Church in Detroit, 1855 (still standing, although not here reproduced). With the Scotsman James Anderson, Albert Jordan planned the memorable Saint John's Church on Woodward Avenue in 1860-1861.

There is only one extant example in Michigan of the work of H. H. Richardson (1838-1886), the Bagley Fountain of 1886 in Detroit, but the essence of the Richardsonian Romanesque that swept the nation in the 1880s and 1890s is perfectly rendered by the J. W. Thompson house of 1895 in Port Huron. The name of the architect is as yet undiscovered, and the temptation is inevitable to consider this an early work of Albert Kahn while a draftsman with Mason & Rice. By 1887 Mason & Rice were finishing the Grand Hotel at Mackinac, one of the rare surviving great summer hotels of the late nineteenth century.

While the New York firm of McKim, Mead & White did not have an extensive practice in Michigan, Detroit possesses a unique specimen of the shingle style which they did so much to make popular on the eastern seacoast. This is the mansion of Whistler's friend Charles Lang Freer on Ferry Avenue, ca. 1887, today the headquarters of the Merrill-Palmer Institute. The architect was Wilson Eyre, Jr. of Philadelphia.

There may not be a superb palace by McKim, Mead & White in Michigan, but the palatial manner for which they were so renowned in their later years is more than adequately represented. "Rose Terrace," the Grosse Pointe residence of Mrs. Horace Dodge, designed by the office of Horace Trumbauer (1868-1938) in 1934, is still standing, although it could not be photographed for this book. It is an endearing advertisement of the Louis XV style that Trumbauer's chief draftsman the Negro Julien Abele handled with such skill. Close at hand are two palaces by another easterner, Charles A. Platt (1861-1933). He referred to the French tradition in the residence of Henry Stephens (1913) and to the Italian in that of Russell A. Alger, Jr. (1910), which today serves as the Grosse Pointe War Memorial. Kahn's eclectic mansions have already been mentioned. One of the better examples of a large country house by a Michigan firm is that of Mrs. Alfred G. Wilson in Rochester, planned in 1929 by Smith, Hinchman & Grylls, who may be better known for their many Detroit skyscrapers, including the Guardian and Penobscot buildings.

The prudent eclecticism of Ralph Adams Cram (1863-1942) was much admired in Michigan. One of his monuments is Saint Paul's Cathedral in Detroit (consecrated 1919). His partner, Bertram Grosvenor Goodhue (1869-1924), was to have built Christ Church, Cranbrook; it was completed after his death by his associates. Another conservative, Cass Gilbert (1858-1934), was selected as the architect of the Detroit Public Library (completed in 1921); still another, Paul-Philippe Cret (1876-1945), was awarded the commission for the Detroit Institute of Arts (dedicated 1927).

In the meantime Frank Lloyd Wright (1869-1959) was not neglected. Although he lost the chance to create "Fairlane," Henry Ford's house at Dearborn, more than a hint of the experimentation that culminated in the Guggenheim Museum in New York City is given by the Curtis Meyer house of 1951 at Galesburg Village, and an extraordinary example of his seemingly simple genius is the W. C. Alpaugh house at Northport. Whether just the nine photographs in this book do justice to the achievement in Michigan of America's greatest architect is an embarrassing question for the author to answer.

But even the most superficial account of modern architecture in this state cannot omit the work of William Buck Stratton (1865-1938), who was intimately associated, as was his wife the former Mary Chase, with the Detroit Society of Arts and Crafts. Stratton may be seen to best advantage in his own house of 1927 in Grosse Pointe, whose subtle unconventionality may not be too far removed from that of the Californian Bernard R. Maybeck.

Nor may Victor Gruen (1903—) be passed over. At Northland and Eastland shopping centers he has attempted with singular success to solve one of the problems peculiar to Detroit, that of providing a community focus for areas that have become all too transient in an era like our own, when wage-earners may be summoned overnight to move out of town.

While it is true that most of the new houses in the Detroit suburbs are remarkable only for their timidity, forcing one to believe that their designers prefer tearooms to restaurants, the architecture of Michigan has an ancient and honorable tradition. One of the accomplishments of Kahn and the Saarinens was to prove in their time that a tradition must not be an end, but only a beginning.

A. 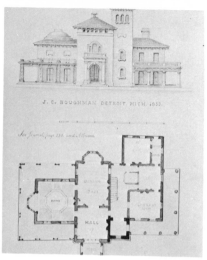 Christopher Reeve, Detroit, 1852
(Alexander Jackson Davis)
Courtesy, Metropolitan Museum
of Art, New York.

B. J. C. Boughman, Detroit, 1853
(Alexander Jackson Davis)
Courtesy, Metropolitan Museum
of Art, New York.

C. Bela Hubbard, Detroit, 1854
(Alexander Jackson Davis)
Courtesy, Metropolitan Museum
of Art, New York.

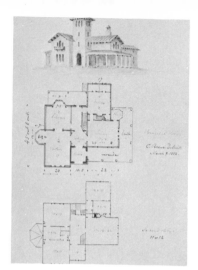

the photographs

MARSHALL

(1) Best known to Michigan residents in 1967 as the site of one of Win Schuler's famous restaurants, Marshall has two other claims to our attention. It *almost* became the capital of the state. It *has* become an architectural capital, for no other town in Michigan offers better examples of houses built in the decades prior to the Civil War, when the Greek and Gothic revivals were flourishing.

Perhaps the finest Greek Revival mansion in Marshall is that erected by Dr. Andrew L. Hays ca. 1838. Its Tuscan colonnade dominates the northwest corner of Prospect and Kalamazoo Streets. In 1924 the property was acquired by Harold C. Brooks, whose brother Louis E. Brooks had the house repaired and restored by the Kalamazoo architect Howard P. Young.

(2) Another good example of the Greek Revival in Marshall is the residence on the northeast corner of Prospect and Kalamazoo streets erected ca. 1840 by the local dry-goods dealer Jabez Fitch. As in the case of the Hays house, there is no record of an architect's being involved, but the builder seems to have been Fitch himself. A native of Unadilla, Otsego County, New York, he may have invented the Ionic colonnade after thumbing through carpenters' handbooks. In our own century the property passed into the hands of Harold C. Brooks, who asked the distinguished Danish-American landscape architect Jens Jensen to lay out the grounds.

(3) Still another example of the Greek revival in Marshall is this house on the southeast corner of Mansion and High streets, built ca. 1842 to please the local jeweler and silversmith Daniel Pratt. Again, there is no record of an architect, but the subtle windows behind the Doric colonnade suggest that the carpenter was a gentleman of taste.

(4) "The Greek temple disease has passed its crisis," observed Andrew Jackson Downing in 1846. "The people have survived it." Downing, a landscape architect of Newburgh, New York, was *the* architectural critic in the days before the Civil War. He fought for a cause, which was the Gothic revival, and a Greek revival mansion rarely appealed to his difficult taste. In Marshall he had many followers, one of whom was Abner Baker, who insisted ca. 1858 on building this Gothic villa on the northeast corner of Mansion and Kalamazoo streets. A porch on the Kalamazoo side has been removed, and the original porch on Mansion has been altered, but enough remains to testify to Downing's profound influence.

(5) Still another Gothic villa was erected in Marshall by Christian Mann in 1861 on the west side of High Street between Prospect and Mansion. Mann was to become the editor of the *Democratic Expounder*.

(6) The so-called "Honolulu House," now the headquarters of the Marshall Historical Society, was erected in 1860 by Abner Pratt, who returned to Marshall in 1859 after serving two years as U. S. Consul to the Sandwich Islands. According to local legend, "Honolulu House" is said to resemble the dwelling Pratt occupied in the islands. This may be the case, but there is no question the designer of the house was influenced by the work of Henry Austin, a New Haven, Connecticut architect of this period, who was fond of planning Italian villas with corbels as ominous as on this porch.

(7) There was no limit to the imagination of carpenters in the nineteenth century, as is proved by this house on the southeast corner of Kalamazoo and Prospect streets, Marshall. Nathan Benedict is said to have erected the original block as early as 1844, but the tower with its pagoda-like pinnacle was not built until after 1857, when the property belonged to Dr. Henry Joy.

GRASS LAKE

(8) One of the most charming examples of the Greek revival in Michigan is "Village Farm," erected ca. 1840 at what is now 971 East Michigan Avenue in Grass Lake. Its Ionic portico indicates that the local carpenter was a diligent student of the best handbooks.

(9) Still another fine example of the Greek revival in Grass Lake is this house, erected in 1840 on Michigan just west of Maute Road by Sidney T. Smith. Its Dorico portico with square Doric columns may well have been inspired by a design in Minard Lafever's *Modern Builder's Guide*, published in 1833.

(10) A tour of the Greek revival in Grass Lake should end with this graceful Ionic colonnade. According to information supplied by the present owner, this house at 425 East Michigan Road may have been erected ca. 1836 by Warren Buckland.

(11) A surprising example of the Gothic revival on Grosse Ile is this residence for Samuel Lewis which may have been erected on East River Road between Macomb and Parkway ca. 1859. The name of the architect has not been recorded, if indeed an architect was employed.

GROSSE ILE

(12) Gordon W. Lloyd was the architect in 1859 of this delightful Gothic villa for Judge (of the Circuit Court) Samuel Townsend Douglas at what is now 24740 East River in Grosse Ile.

13) The Gothic revival is well illustrated on Grosse Ile, where Gordon
W. Lloyd (1832-1904) designed
Saint James Episcopal Church in
1867.

ANN ARBOR

(14) A certain Christopher Grossman may have been the first owner of this Gothic villa at 1020 West Huron Street, Ann Arbor. It may have been erected as early as 1853. Since this photograph was taken, the house has been altered.

(15) What may be the most splendid Greek revival house in Ann Arbor was erected in 1843 by Judge Robert S. Wilson at 126 North Division Street.

TECUMSEH

(16) Although old St. Peter's Episcopal Church was recently destroyed to satisfy the apostles of progress, the trace of the Greek revival has not yet been entirely eliminated in Tecumseh. This villa at 501 West Chicago boulevard is said to have been erected in 1849 by Rhoda Pitts Bacon.

(17) Another example of the Greek revival in Tecumseh is the residence erected in 1832 by Elijah Anderson at 401 West Chicago Boulevard.

WASHINGTON

(18) The vogue for octagonal houses was launched in 1849 when Orson Squire Fowler and his brother Lorenzo published *A Home for all; or, the Gravel Wall, and Octagon Mode of Building*. Until that time Orson Squire Fowler had been famous as a frantic phrenologist. He was the author of *Love and Parentage, applied to the Improvement of Offspring, including Important Directions and Suggestions to Lovers and the Married concerning the Strongest Ties and the Most Momentous Relations of Life*, which had gone through 40 printings by 1844. So had its sequel: *Evils and Remedies of Excessive and Perverted Sexuality, including Warning and Advice to the Married and Single*.

This example at 5763 Van Dyke Avenue, Washington, was erected in 1860 by Loren Andrus, an engineer who surveyed the Clinton and Kalamazoo Canal and the route of the railroad between Port Huron and Flint. The architect was Andrus's brother-in-law the local carpenter David Stewart. In 1964 the property was sold to Wayne State University, and is now headquarters of the Albert H. Schmidt Foundation Farm for Wayne students specializing in agriculture.

DEXTER

(19) Judge Samuel W. Dexter erected this mansion with its Doric portico on Dexter Road 1841-43.

MANCHESTER

(20) This Gothic villa for Jabez Fountain on the southwest corner of City and Summit streets in Manchester was apparently erected ca. 1853.

(21) This brick house for Dr. Amariah Conklin at 224 Ann Arbor Road, possibly built ca. 1853, gives a good idea of the high standards of Manchester's brick-builders and masons before the Civil War.

IONIA

(22) America's very first Italian villa (another popular style prior to the Civil War) seems to have been the residence of Bishop George W. Doane at Burlington, New Jersey, designed by John Notman in 1837. One of the best examples in Michigan is the present Hall-Fowler Library at 126 East Main Street in Ionia. It was erected in 1860 as the home of the local banker Frederick Hall. Captain Lucius Mills was the builder.

DETROIT

(23) Gordon W. Lloyd was not the only Detroit architect in the middle years of the nineteenth century who specialized in Gothic revival churches. The brothers Octavius and Albert H. Jordan (from Hartford, Connecticut) were responsible for the distinguished Fort Street Presbyterian Church of 1855, still standing at 631 West Fort Street. Octavius Jordan soon returned to Hartford, but his brother Albert H. Jordan joined forces with the Scotsman James Anderson to design St. John's Episcopal Church (above), on the southwest corner of Vernor and Woodward Avenue in 1860-61.

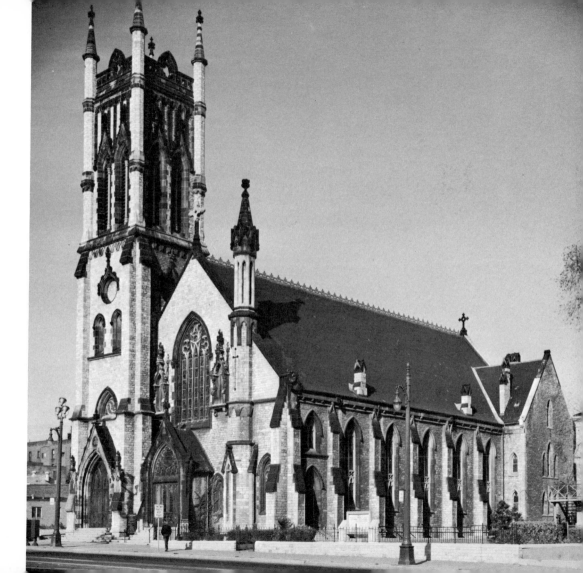

DETROIT

(24) One of the larger commissions of the Gothic revivalist Gordon W. Lloyd was Christ Church, on Jefferson Avenue (to the east of the Chrysler Expressway, Detroit) erected 1861-63.

MACKINAC ISLAND

(25) One of the rare surviving examples of the great summer hotels of the late nineteenth century is the Grand Hotel, Mackinac Island, designed by the firm of Mason & Rice in 1887.

PORT HURON

(26) Perhaps the finest example in Michigan of Richardson's influence is this mansion at 1719 Military Road, Port Huron, erected in 1895 by John W. Thompson. The name of the architect has not been preserved. In 1967 it is serving as the headquarters of the Eastern Michigan College of Commerce.

DETROIT

(27) Henry Hobson Richardson (1838-1886) was the genius who transformed American architecture after the Civil War, bringing order out of chaos by simplifying massing. His Trinity Church, Boston, a free translation of the Romanesque in granite trimmed with freestone, enchanted a generation. His only surviving work in Michigan is the Bagley Memorial Fountain in Grand Circus Park, Detroit, 1885. The Republican John Judson Bagley, who had grown rich in the tobacco business, was elected governor of Michigan in 1872 and again in 1874.

The MERRILL-PALMER SCHOOL
ADMINISTRATION OFFICE NO. 71

(28) The finest example in Michigan of the so-called "Shingle Style," originated by Henry Hobson Richardson and exploited with the utmost success on the east coast by McKim, Mead & White, is the residence of Charles Lang Freer (1856-1919) at 71 East Ferry Avenue, erected ca. 1887 to the designs of Wilson Eyre, Jr. In 1967 the Freer mansion is serving as the headquarters of the Merrill-Palmer School, Detroit, founded 1920 under the will of Lizzie Merrill Palmer, widow of Senator Thomas W. Palmer.

Freer, a native of Kingston, New York, who grew rich as one of the directors of the Michigan Car Company, specializing in ore, refrigerator, and coal cars for the railroads, was one of the outstanding art collectors of the late nineteenth century. His collection of Oriental art is now housed in the Freer Gallery of Art in Washington, D. C., as is his matchless collection of the work of his friend James McNeill Whistler. Whistler's "Peacock Room," now in the Freer Gallery in Washington, originally commissioned by Frederick Leyland of London, could once be seen in the annex to this house on Ferry Avenue.

(29) The Detroit Club, whose first president was Charles Freer's partner Hugh McMillan, opened this building on the northeast corner of Cass and Fort streets in 1892. The architect was Wilson Eyre, Jr. Its round-arched windows look back to the Richardsonian Romanesque, but the renaissance revival epitomized by the Chicago World's Fair of 1893 is obviously in the offing.

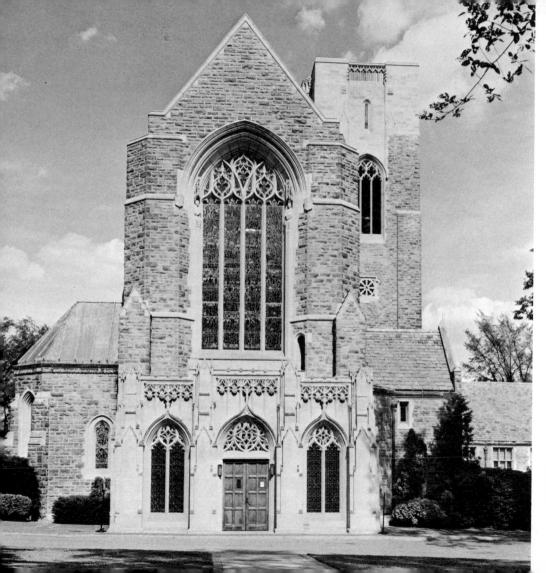

(30) St. Paul's (Episcopal) Cathedral at 4800 Woodward Avenue (dedicated 1911, consecrated 1919) is the major achievement in the Detroit area of Ralph Adams Cram (1863-1942). "In Saint Paul's Cathedral," wrote Cram, "an attempt has been made to adapt to modern ideals, conditions and environment that style of architecture which Christian civilization developed for its own expression, the so-called Gothic of the Middle Ages. . . . Recourse has been had to that early type of thirteenth-century work represented by Tetley and Tintern Abbeys." Cram was disappointed that his design was left unfinished. "As the building now stands," he made plain, "without its central tower, it is lacking in both form and consistency."

Against the "modernist idea" in the field of art Cram stood firm. "It has its own place and it may and should go to it," he decided. "Its boundaries are definite and fixed, and beyond them it cannot go, for the Angel of Decency, Propriety and Reason stands there with a flaming sword."

BLOOMFIELD HILLS

(31) Cram's partner Bertram Grosvenor Goodhue (1869-1924) was to have designed Christ Church Cranbrook at 470 Church Road, Bloomfield Hills, in the rather archaeological Gothic style beloved by the partners of Cram, Goodhue & Ferguson. On Goodhue's death, the project was carried forward and completed by Bertram Grosvenor Goodhue Associates.

DETROIT

(32) Cass Gilbert (1859-1934), best remembered for the Woolworth Building in New York City and the Minnesota State Capital, left his mark on Detroit with the Detroit Public Library, 5201 Woodward Avenue, whose white Vermont marble facade testifies to Gilbert's long study of the Italian Renaissance, both in his student years in Italy and in his apprenticeship in New York with the firm of McKim, Mead, & White. The original building, begun in 1917, was completed in 1921. The Cass Avenue addition, the work of Cass Gilbert, Jr., Francis J. Keally, and the W. B. Ford Associates, was begun in 1960 and completed in 1965.

(33) Paul-Philippe Cret (1876-1945), a native of Lyons, France, and a graduate of the Ecole des Beaux Arts, was the principal architect of the main building of the Detroit Institute of Arts at 5200 Woodward Avenue (dedicated 1927). His associates were the Philadelphia firm of Zantziger, Borie, & Medary, with whom he collaborated on the Indianapolis Public Library, and who did much of the work on the Philadelphia Museum of Art. The South Wing of the Museum, opened in 1966, was both tactful and modern, the work of Harley, Ellington, Cowin & Stirton, with Gunnar Birkerts as design consultant.

GRAND RAPIDS

(34) America's greatest architect, Frank Lloyd Wright (1869-1959), cannot be said to have neglected Michigan. In 1909, the very year in which he finished the famous Robie house in Chicago, he designed this house for Meyer S. May at 450 Madison Avenue S. E. in Grand Rapids.

(35) Although Frank Lloyd Wright obtained the commission for this residence of David Amberg at 505 College Avenue, Grand Rapids, the building was designed and completed during Wright's absence in Europe by Hermann V. von Holst and Marion Mahony (later the wife of the Chicago architect Walter Burley Griffin). Amberg was the father-in-law of Meyer S. May. This was the period in which Wright won—and lost—the commission for "Fairlane," Henry Ford's house at Dearborn.

BLOOMFIELD HILLS

(36) One of the remarkable advertisements of Wright's genius in the neighborhood of Detroit is this house for Melvyn Maxwell Smith at 5045 Pon Valley Road, Bloomfield Hills, erected 1951.

NORTHPORT

(37) In the open country on a hill north of Northport stands this house which Frank Lloyd Wright designed in 1951 for Mrs. W. C. Alpaugh of Cincinnati. The addition on the left is the work of Glen T. Arat & Associates.

ANN ARBOR

(38) Frank Lloyd Wright designed this house in 1951 for William Palmer at 227 Orchard Hills Drive, Ann Arbor.

(39) A view of the dining room of the William Palmer house by Frank Lloyd Wright (1951) at 227 Orchard Hills Drive.

SAINT JOSEPH

(40) Frank Lloyd Wright completed this house for Carl E. Schultz, 2704 Highland Court, Saint Joseph, in 1959, the year of his death.

(41) Balcony of the Carl E. Schultz house.

(42) Frank Lloyd Wright designed this residence for Mrs. Ina M. Harper on Lake Shore Road, Saint Joseph, in 1951.

(43) The experimentation that led to the final design of the Guggenheim Museum, New York City, is quite evident in this cinder-block residence of Curtis Meyer at 11108 Hawthorne Drive, Galesburg Village, designed by Frank Lloyd Wright in 1951. Galesburg Village outside of Kalamazoo is one of the three Wright "colonies" in Michigan. Parkwyn Village near Kalamazoo and the cluster of houses in Okemos should also be cited.

GALESBURG VILLAGE

KALAMAZOO

MIDLAND

(44) Alfonso Iannelli (1888-1965), a native of Andretta, Italy, was one of the two sculptors (the other was Richard W. Bock) who collaborated with Frank Lloyd Wright on his famous Midway Gardens in Chicago, 1913. In 1937 Iannelli created this Fountain of the Pioneers for Bronson Square in Kalamazoo.

(45) One of the most famous graduates of Frank Lloyd Wright's Taliesin Fellowship is Alden B. Dow (1904—). Much of his work may be seen in Midland, headquarters of the Dow Chemical Company, where he built this residence for himself at 315 Post Street in 1935.

(46) A view of the lakeside pavilion of the Alden B. Dow house at 315 Post Street, Midland, designed by Alden B. Dow in 1935.

BLOOMFIELD HILLS

(47) "Cranbrook House," at 500 Lone Pine Road in Bloomfield Hills, originally the home of George Gough Booth and his wife (the former Ellen Warner Scripps), is now used as a center for the Episcopal Church. It was designed in 1909 by Albert Kahn (1869-1942) whose success in building factories should lead no one to overlook his skill in domestic work. He may have been inspired in this instance by the precedents of his English contemporary Sir Edwin Landseer Lutyens.

DETROIT

(48) The great Chicago architect Daniel Hudson Burnham had already shown what might be accomplished with the classical revival for business buildings when Albert Kahn in 1920 created this complex for General Motors at the southeast corner of West Grand and Second boulevards, Detroit. But Kahn proved he could rival Burnham himself in this building, conceived at the very moment William Crapo Durant was losing control of GM, and Pierre S. du Pont was about to become president.

(49) This closeup of the fenestration of the old Ford Motor Co. Sales Building on the northwest corner of West Grand and Woodward, Detroit, designed by Albert Kahn in 1913, gives some indication of his skill in handling terra cotta for a business building facade. Since this photograph was taken the building has been altered beyond recognition.

(50) Albert Kahn's genius as a city planner has not yet been given due recognition, but in 1928 when his firm designed the Fisher Building on the northwest corner of West Grand and Second boulevards, he anticipated with amazing shrewdness the needs of the growing city. The spacious shopping arcade, the theater (in which plays bound for Broadway try out) and the generous office space for the medical profession emphasize his profoundly practical ambition. Nearby in 1931 he built (again for the Fisher Brothers of GM) the New Center Building now housing the Detroit store of Saks Fifth Avenue.

ANN ARBOR

(51) The campus of the University of Michigan would be inconceivable without the talent of Albert Kahn who in 1918 completed this General Library Building. In its austerity—and its dignity—it recalls the greater achievements of the Chicago architect Dwight Heald Perkins, who was responsible for Carl Schurz School on Chicago's northwest side.

(52) The Hill Auditorium on the Michigan Campus (on North University Avenue between Thayer and Ingalls Streets) was designed by Albert Kahn in 1913 in collaboration with Ernest Wilby. As in the adjacent University Library, Kahn shows that he never neglected the work of his contemporaries in the Chicago School—particularly that of Dwight H. Perkins.

(53) Kahn's favorite of all the buildings he designed was the William L. Clements Library of American History on the Michigan campus, opened in 1923. If he had been in search of a precedent he could easily have found a model in the Morgan Library, New York, built by McKim, Mead & White in 1906. Kahn saw no reason to apologize for his reverence for the Italian Renaissance, so evident here and in many other of his creations.

GROSSE POINTE

(54) Perhaps the most splendid of all Albert Kahn's domestic commissions was the mansion he designed in 1929 in the Cotswold manner for Mr. & Mrs. Edsel B. Ford, Grosse Pointe Shores. In this view the mansion is shown looking toward Saint Clair Shores.

(55) In this photo of the Edsel B. Ford residence, the view shows the house from the edge of Lake Saint Clair.

(56) The Danish-born landscape architect Jens Jensen (1860-1951), who frequently collaborated with Frank Lloyd Wright, had the opportunity of planning this grove of trees leading up to the Ford estate.

(57) This cove on Lake Saint Clair was laid out by Jens Jensen for the Ford estate.

(58) Another memorable achievement of Albert Kahn was this mansion for the late Alvan Macauley at 735 Lake Shore Road, Grosse Point Shores, completed in 1930. From 1916 to 1939 Mr. Macauley was president of the Packard Motor Car Co. From 1939 to 1948 he was chairman of the board.

WARREN

(59) Albert Kahn's factories, such has been the expansion of Detroit as an industrial center, have been subject to constant alteration and at times to obliteration. One of his outstanding factory designs was this Dodge Half-Ton Truck Plant at 21500 Mound Road in Warren, dating from 1938. Since this photo was taken radical changes have been made.

GROSSE POINTE

(60) One of the really unusual early modern houses in Michigan is this casual, unassuming brick dwelling at 938 Three Mile Drive, Grosse Pointe Park. It was built in 1927 by the architect William Buck Stratton (1865-1938) as a home for himself and his wife the talented ceramist Mary Chase Stratton (1867-1961). Mrs. Stratton, who headed the Pewabic Pottery at 10125 East Jefferson Avenue, Detroit (the building was designed by her husband), was a member of the first executive committee of the Detroit Society of Arts and Crafts. Stratton himself led the committee and (with architect H. J. Maxwell Grylls) designed the old home of the Society on Watson Street off Woodward. Stratton was also responsible for the Women's City Club, the Naval Armory, and the Belle Isle Bath House. On Three Mile Drive Stratton realized a house which might have charmed even that most imaginative Californian, Bernard R. Maybeck.

(61) In 1913 Charles A. Platt (1861-1933) designed this mansion at 241 Lake Shore Road, Grosse Pointe Farms, for the lumber magnate Henry Stephens. While not forgetting the precedents of Georgian architecture in America, Platt recalled in the attenuated windows here the eighteenth century in France.

(62) "The Moorings" at 32 Lake Shore Road, Grosse Pointe Farms, was created in 1910 by Charles Adams Platt (1861-1933) for Russell A. Alger, Jr., son of McKinley's Secretary of War. It was one of the three commanding Italian palaces by this architect in the Middle West. "Villa Turicum," the estate of Edith Rockefeller McCormick in Lake Forest, Illinois, has been demolished, but "Gwinn," the residence of William Gwinn Mather, is still standing in Cleveland, Ohio. Today "The Moorings" serves as the Grosse Pointe War Memorial.

ROCHESTER

(63) View from the gardens of "Meadowbrook Hall," the Tudor residence of the lumber magnate Alfred G. Wilson at 480 South Adams Road, Rochester, erected in 1929 to the plans of Smith, Hinchman & Grylls, famous for their Detroit skyscrapers (including the Penobscot and the Guardian buildings).

(64) Another view of the Tudor residence "Meadowbrook Hall."

BLOOMFIELD HILLS

(65) The arcade of the Cranbrook Academy of Art in Bloomfield Hills was completed by Eero Saarinen (1873-1950) in 1940.

(66) The Swedish sculptor Carl Milles (1875-1955) created this Orpheus Fountain for Cranbrook in 1936. From 1931 to 1950 he was resident sculptor and head of the department of sculpture at Cranbrook Academy.

(67) This tower of the Cranbrook School for Boys was designed by Eliel Saarinen in 1925.

(68) The studios of the Cranbrook Academy of Art were conceived by Eliel Saarinen in 1931-1932.

(69) The Kingswood School for Girls at Cranbrook, which may be the best of all Eliel Saarinen's designs in America, was planned in 1929

(70) Staircase, Kingswood School for Girls, Bloomfield Hills. The statue of Europa and the bull is the work of Carl Milles.

(71) Detail of a column in the arcade of the Kingswood School for Girls.

(72) Library of the Kingswood School for Girls. Loja (Mrs. Eliel) Saarinen was responsible, with the assistance of Maija Wirde, for the rugs.

(73) Dining Hall, Kingswood School for Girls. Loja Saarinen was the artist who created the tapestry in this room.

(74) The Cranbrook Institute of Science was designed by Eliel Saarinen
in 1931.

FENTON

(75) The Fenton Community Center of 1937 at 150 South Leroy
Street was the joint design of Eliel and Eero Saarinen.

WARREN

(76) Eliel Saarinen was to have designed the immense General Motors Technical Center at Mound Road and Twelve Mile in Warren, and he did make sketches as early as 1945. But the planning did not begin in earnest until 1948 and, by 1950, on his father's death, Eero Saarinen (1910-1961) was in complete charge, associated with the Detroit firm of Smith, Hinchman & Grylls. Work did not come to an end until 1956.

This view is of the Styling Building. Here as elsewhere at the center Eero Saarinen proved he could be as meticulous as Miës van der Rohe (whom he much admired) but far more imaginative. Calling on the advice of the designer Alexander Girard, the architect eliminated the threat of bleakness by tinting the glazed ceramic sand-moulded bricks in the most stimulating hues. One building may be burnt orange, another bright blue.

It is interesting that the GM executive supervising the project, LeRoy E. Kiefer, was trained as an architect by the older Saarinen at the University of Michigan. Eliel Saarinen spent two years there before moving to Cranbrook.

The General Motors Technical Center may be the most magnificent and the most sensible monument ever erected by a giant corporation.

(77) This view of the entrance to the Styling Building of the GM Technical Center includes a statue by Antoine Pevsner (1884—). The American sculptor Alexander Calder (1898—) was fortunately prevailed upon to design a "water ballet" at the pool in the opposite end of the project.

(78) The Research Staff Building, GM Technical Center.

(79) This is the staircase in the first floor of the Styling Building of the GM Technical Center.

(80) Heavy Test Building, GM Technical Center.

(81) Dynanometer Building, GM Technical Center.

(82) Service Section, GM Technical Center.

(83) Engineering Building, GM Technical Center.

TECHNICAL CENTER
SERVICE SECTION

(84) Close-up of the Engineering Building, GM Technical Center.

(85) Manufacturing Development Building, GM Technical Center.

ANN ARBOR

(86) Eero Saarinen Associates completed this Music Building for the University of Michigan in 1965, four years after his death.

(87) Side view of the Music Building, University of Michigan.

DETROIT

(88) Backed by the financier Herbert S. Greenwald, Ludwig Miës van der Rohe
(1886—), who headed the Bauhaus in Germany on the retirement of Walter Gropius,
was able to design these high rise apartments, completed 1961, for the Lafayette
Park housing development in Detroit. The meticulousness of Miës was an inspiration
to Eero Saarinen while creating the General Motors Technical Center.

(89) A group of the town houses in the Lafayette Park development, 1961, designed
by Ludwig Miës van der Rohe.

GROSSE POINTE

(90) The Grosse Pointe Public Library, the gift of the late Dexter M. Ferry, Jr., was opened at 10 Kercheval Road, Grosse Pointe Farms, in 1953, complete with a mobile by the sculptor Alexander Calder. The architect was the Hungarian-born Marcel Breuer (1902—). Once the associate of Walter Gropius at the Bauhaus in Germany, Breuer joined Gropius again in 1938 at the Harvard School of Design.

SOUTHFIELD

(91) Minoru Yamasaki (1912—), a native of Seattle who became chief architectural designer for Smith, Hinchman & Grylls in 1945, designed this screened palace for the headquarters of the Reynolds Metals Company at 16200 Northland Drive, Southfield, in 1959.

DETROIT

(92) Yamasaki's most famous building in Michigan may be the McGregor Community Center Building at Wayne State University, opened in 1958.

(93) Interior, the McGregor Community Center, Wayne State University, by Minoru Yamasaki & Associates. The building was named for Tracy W. McGregor, an investor in Detroit real estate who was president of the Merrill-Palmer Institute.

(94) The Michigan Consolidated Gas Company at One Woodward Avenue, opened in 1962, is the only Detroit skyscraper so far designed by Minoru Yamasaki & Associates.

(95) Detail, first story, the Michigan Consolidated Gas Company Building by Minoru Yamasaki & Associates, 1962.

HARPER WOODS

(96) The Viennese Victor Gruen (1903—) drew the plans for Eastland Shopping Center at Harper Woods, erected 1955-57. The lion is the work of the Detroit sculptor Marshall Fredericks (1908—).

SOUTHFIELD

(97) Perhaps the most successful of Gruen's Detroit shopping centers is Northland, in Southfield, opened in 1954. The sculptor of the elephant was Arthur Kraft.

ROCHESTER

(98) The tradition of Eliel Saarinen is maintained in our time by Swanson Associates, who completed Saint John Fisher Chapel at 3665 Walton Boulevard, Rochester, in 1966. J. Robert F. Swanson, the head of the firm, studied under Eliel Saarinen at Ann Arbor and married his daughter Pipsan.

(99) Interior, Saint John Fisher Chapel, by Swanson Associates, 1966.

OLIVET

(100) This Student Center at Olivet College was opened in 1962. Its designers were the firm of Meathe, Kessler Associates, founded by Philip J. Meathe (1924—), a native of Grosse Pointe, and William Kessler (1924—), a native of Reading, Pennsylvania. Meathe was trained at the University of Michigan, while Kessler is a graduate of the Institute of Design, Chicago, and the Harvard School of Architecture.

MOUNT CLEMENS

(101) The Mount Clemens Federal Savings Building at 77 South Gratiot was completed in 1961 by Meathe, Kessler Associates.

GROSSE POINTE

(102) In 1964 Meathe, Kessler completed this house for W. Hawkins Ferry and his collection of modern art at 874 Lake Shore Road, Grosse Pointe Shores.

(103) A view from Lake Saint Clair of the W. Hawkins Ferry residence.

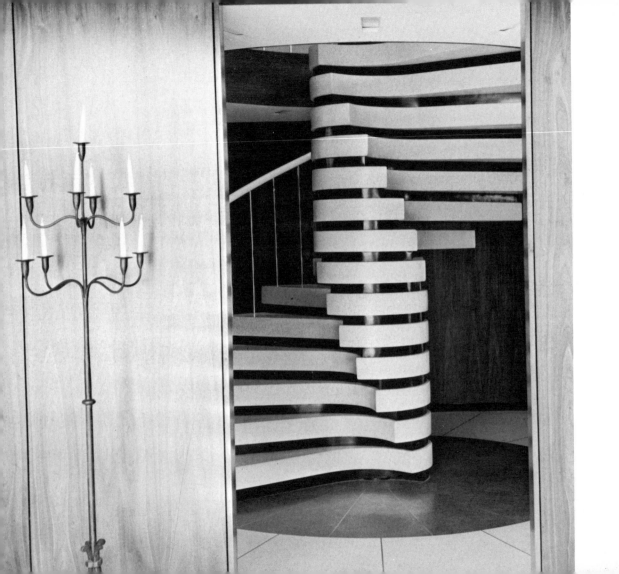

(104) Interior of the front hall of the W. Hawkins Ferry residence.

MANISTEE

(105) This casual summer cottage for Judge John B. Swainson (Governor of Michigan 1961-63) and his brother-in-law Patrick Whitehead, on the grounds of the Professional Club near Manistee, was completed by Meathe, Kessler Associates in 1966. It may be the most distinguished house built in Michigan since the end of the second world war.

BIBLIOGRAPHY

Christ-Janer, Albert, *Eliel Saarinen*, Chicago, 1948.

Colby, Joy Hakanson, *Art And A City*, Detroit, 1966.

Cooper, Mabel Ruth, *Nineteenth Century Homes of Marshall, Michigan*, Unpublished doctoral dissertation, Florida State University, Tallahassee, 1963.

Eaton, Leonard K., *Landscape Artist in America: The Life and Work of Jens Jensen*, Chicago, 1965.

Ferry, W. Hawkins, "Representative Detroit Buildings: A Cross Section of Architecture 1823-1943," *Bulletin of the Detroit Institute of Arts*, March, 1943.

Ferry, W. Hawkins, "The Gothic and Tuscan Revivals in Detroit: 1828-1875," *Art Quarterly*, Summer, 1946.

Ferry, W. Hawkins, "The Mansions of Grosse Pointe," *Monthly Bulletin of the Michigan Society of Architects*, March, 1956.

Griggs, Joseph, "The Prairie Spirit in Architecture," *Prairie School Review*, Fourth Quarter, 1965.

McKee, Harley J., "Glimpses of Architecture—Michigan," *Michigan History*, March, 1966.

McLean, Evelyn G., *Some Notable Alumni of Cranbrook Academy*, Unpublished master's essay, Wayne State University, Detroit, 1966.

Nelson, George, *The Industrial Architecture of Albert Kahn*, New York, 1939.

Pickens, Buford L., "Treasure Hunting at Detroit," *Architectural Review*, December, 1944.

Saarinen, Aline B., editor, *Eero Saarinen On His Work*, New Haven, 1962.

Taylor, Howell, "Michigan's Pioneer Architecture," *Michigan History*, March, 1953.

Temko, Allan, *Eero Saarinen*, New York, 1962.

Van Zanten, David T., "The Early Work of Marion Mahony Griffin," *Prairie School Review*, Second Quarter, 1966.

Woodward, William T., illustrator, *A Tour Guide To Grosse Ile*, Grosse Ile Historical Society, Grosse Ile, 1963.

Woolfenden, William E., *A Study of Nineteenth Century Church Architecture in Detroit, Michigan*, Unpublished master's thesis, Wayne State University, Detroit, 1941.

A native of Kenilworth, Illinois, Wayne Andrews is a graduate of the Winnetka Public Schools, Lawrenceville School, Harvard (A.B. 1936) and Columbia (Ph.D. 1956). Since 1964 he has been Archives of American Art Professor at Wayne State University. He is the author of *The Vanderbilt Legend*, 1941, *Battle for Chicago*, 1946, *Architecture, Ambition and Americans*, 1955, *Architecture in America*, 1960, *Germaine: A Portrait of Madame de Staël*, 1963, and the forthcoming *Architecture in Chicago and Mid-America*, to be published by Atheneum in 1968. Under the pseudonym Montagu O'Reilly he is also the author of *Who Has Been Tampering With These Pianos*, 1948, and he is the editor of *The Best Stories of Edith Wharton*, 1957, and *Concise Dictionary of American History*, 1962. Before joining the Wayne faculty he was curator of manuscripts at the New York Historical Society and an editor at Charles Scribner's Sons. He has contributed to the *New York Times Book Review*, the *Saturday Review*, the *Architectural Review*, *House & Garden*, *House Beautiful*, *Town & Country*, *Harper's Bazaar*, *Harper's* and other magazines.

The manuscript was edited by Ralph Busick. The book was designed by Donald Ross. The type faces for the book are I.B.M.'s Modern (based on Univers) and Venus designed by Bauer, 1907-1913.

The book is printed on Hooper's Sunray Vellum. The paperback book is bound in Riegal's Carolina cover, and the hardcover edition is bound in Columbia Mills' Bayside Vellum. Manufactured in the United States of America.